Captain,
TITANIC
& Me
ROSE GALLAGHER

YouCaxton Publications

132 Frankwell, Shrewsbury, Shropshire. SY3 8JX
www.youCaxton.co.uk

Published in Great Britain by
YouCaxton 2012

ISBN 978-0-9571454-4-3

Contents

Introduction

Captain Edward John Smith 'The millionaires' Captain' a kind and loving Family Man. I want to take you on a journey, a walk in the shoes of Captain Edward John Smith. Look through his eyes, and share his world, be a part of his life and his family; remember him as a hugely popular man. A man who commanded respect with simply a contagious smile! Sit yourself down by the fire, men folk withdraw to the smoking room to enjoy a Havana cigar, creating plumes of swirling blue smoke, whilst the ladies enjoy a tipple and read beautiful poetry written by Alfred, Lord Tennyson, Poet Laureate of England in 1896.

Eleanor Smith loved reading, a pastime that would always entertain her guests. Get to know the man, the husband and the father. It took over 20 years to write this and the 100 year anniversary of the Titanic's disastrous demise to encourage me to put pen to paper. Because this isn't just Captain Edward John Smith's house – it's my house, and it will always hold a special place in my heart. What compulsion drew me to this place? Why me? It was meant to be – it's that simple, *I had a dream …*

A child of the potteries and a farmer's daughter … Let's meet two children whose place in history was already mapped out. Sarah Eleanor was born in Liverpool to Sarah and William Pennington in 1861. Edward John was born to Catherine and John Smith in Stoke on Trent 1850. Edward was keen to go to sea and in 1863 at the tender age of 13 he left for Liverpool to start an apprenticeship on the Senator Weber owned by A. Gibson & Co. of Liverpool. This was to be the start of an amazing journey, and he would swiftly earn his pathway to joining the White Star Line in 1880.

The Path to Marine Crescent

Young Captain Smith

It was such an amazing time for Edward John Smith: not only had he achieved goals that most of us could only dream of, such as sailing to places like Australia and New York – but with grizzled determination he had fulfilled his aspiration to reach great heights in his career - making lasting friendships along the way. He was about to embark on a new and exciting episode of his personal life, one that would happily last for the rest of his days.

He met, fell in love, and married the beautiful Sarah Eleanor Pennington on Tuesday July 12th 1887 in Winwick Parish Church, Warrington.

Initially setting up home near Tuebrook, they soon moved to one of the more wealthier parts of Liverpool to be closer to the docks.

That move took them to 17 Marine Crescent, Waterloo, telephone number Waterloo 271. The family moved house in 1898 and it was in this year that Helen Melville Smith, their first and only child, was born on 2nd April 1898

It was here in 1903 that Captain Smith wrote his will, leaving everything to his wife Eleanor, or, in the event of her re-marriage, to their daughter, Helen Melville.

King Edward VII

King Edward VII awards Captain Smith the Transport Medal. When the Boer War started in 1899, the Majestic was called upon to transport the troops to Cape Colony. Captain Smith made two trips to South Africa and for his service King Edward VII awarded him the Transport Medal, showing the "South Africa" clasp. How proud the family must have been. Just imagine the parties, what celebrations afterwards!

If only walls could talk …

Take A Tour And Walk In Captain Smiths Shoes

Come with me and see what Edward and Eleanor saw... and what I still see today... The old wrought iron garden gate opens wide, with a distinctive 'clang' sound as the latch strikes against the gudgeon set fast into the sandstone pillars as it closes safely behind. A sound easily recognised even from inside the house.

17 Marine Crescent 1898

The same sound that resonates today in 2012 and has done so for the past 190 years. The blacksmith who forged the garden gate proudly displayed signage to advertise his skills, a lasting testimony to the quality of workmanship of the day. You can still clearly see the sign:

'WORRAL & Co' 26 Byron St, Liverpool

Those of you who delight in preservation will enjoy the meticulous detail and the handsome décor of the exterior of the house, with tasteful Victorian intricate individual wrought iron supports that weave their way up to the veranda roof. Walking toward the house and front door, clasp the old 'Victorian Beehive' door knob used by the whole family to enter their home. The original door furniture is still on the front door and can be seen today. As you walk through the vestibule, raise your eyes to the delicate rose carvings above the door, making a very handsome feature for the entrance. Most beautiful of all are the hand painted red roses that adorn the wooden floor. Was this Eleanor's artwork? She may very well have painted them: I like to think so.

The main family staircase lies ahead of you, the stairs leading to six bedrooms arranged around a bright central hall. A master bedroom, guest rooms and a nursery.

In the 1830s houses for the rich were built with such decadence. With large bright rooms and very high ceilings with decorative cornices, this house is typical of the era, boasting a drawing room, dining room, study and a smoking room where the gentlemen would withdraw after dinner.

Captain Smith loved to smoke his Havana cigars, as his daughter, Mel, recalls later in this book.

Of course a home would not be complete without the servants, and the Smith home was no exception. The Census records for 1901 list the Parlour Maid as Annie Brett, just 17 years old, and the Domestic Cook as Kate Chambers, aged 32, from Ireland.

There was a kitchen and a scullery, with servants' quarters above: here the staff would eat their meals and enjoy their leisure time.

The basement (which had been sealed over before I moved here, and intriguingly still remains unopened to this day – what mysteries lie within?) it would probably have been a wine cellar in days gone by..

This house boasts two staircases, however the one in the kitchen would only be used by servants, for access to their living quarters (fondly referred to as the 'west wing'). The servants would share a room which would have been sparsely furnished.

In Victorian times, servants would never use the front door, but the tradesmen's entrance at the back of the house, close to the stables, where deliveries of food and coal would also be made.

In 1898, when Helen Melville (later, she chose to be called 'Mel') was born, the large back bedroom became the nursery with its huge white marble fireplace and black ornate cast insert, the largest, warmest fire in the house! The entrance to this room has a really strange tiny doorway: DUCK your head as you walk through! No doubt there have been a few sore heads over time -I should know, as even now I still forget and have had a sore head many times to show for it.

The master bedroom was adjacent to the nursery, allowing Eleanor to be close to Mel should she wake in the middle of the night. A master bedroom with a fine, uninterrupted view of the River Mersey.

Eleanor could sit with Mel and nurse her back to sleep, watching through the window the twinkling lights of the ships that pass through the night on the Mersey. No doubt she would be thinking about her husband, who was away at sea on the Majestic taking troops to Cape Colony, South Africa, in 1899.

A little known house guest, and one seldom recorded, was Eleanor's mother, Sarah Pennington, who lived here with the family in one of the many guest rooms. A welcome pair of hands with a new arrival and no doubt a shoulder to cry on when Ted was away for long periods at sea, as he so often was.

Move forward to 1903: the term on the Majestic has come to an end and Ted is back with his family. Close your eyes and imagine the parties, celebrations and socialising in these entertaining rooms.

Imagine the guest list.

The men wearing their double breasted black jackets, with crisp white shirts and black ties, meticulously well kept shiny shoes and neatly trimmed beards or moustaches. All well spoken, polite, knowledgeable and yes gentlemanly. The women, representing home, hearth and family would put on their finery with tall hats and bustle dresses made of silk and handmade embroidered shoes. The women were revered above all things in Victorian times.

Parlour games were a popular pastime of the day

An extract from a book of *Unique Party Games* dated 1890

Bears Game – Here is a game that will break down any icy 'reserve' in seconds. To begin with, put a bun on a plate on the floor in the middle of the room, then ask the whole company to stand around in a circle, with a good space between each person. You do all this with a certain amount of mystery, so as to make everybody wonder what is coming next. Then you announce that you are going to assign the role of an animal to each individual. Thereupon you go round and whisper to everybody in turn the name of some beast or other and you are careful to point out that the names shall be kept secret. Having gone through these preparations, you say "now I'm going to call out the name of an animal and the person who has been allotted the animal I call, must grab the bun before I count five". "Ready", you say and then you shout "Bear". The whole company darts at the bun and there is a delightful mix up on the floor. You see you gave everyone the role of "Bear" that's why. The shrieks of laughter that generally ensues sends all reserve to the four winds.

Those rooms, so full of fun and laughter in those days, are all laid out in an interesting arrangement which seemed so strangely familiar to me when it was my turn to move in…

Just Imagine if you will…

A wonderful array of English summer flowers, the intense scent of lavender and the aroma of the roses scattered all around the garden's borders.

Some can still be seen in the garden, including the rambling rose on the veranda, the lavender, rosemary and the magnificent holly bush.

With some of these flowers and plants surviving today, it's not difficult for me to use my imagination as I use my garden, and theirs.

Lavender with its restful qualities, would be gathered and sewn into lace sachets and placed under the pillows to aid a quiet night's sleep. 'Rosemary', derived from the Latin, Rosmarinus, translates to 'Dew of the Sea'. It grows with little water, as it takes the humidity carried on the sea breeze to live, it grows in my garden today as it has for the past 100 years.

In keeping with tradition I still gather bunches of lavender to hang in the house. I'm not sure if I will ever try to match the Victorians with their lace sachets, however, lavender or rosemary bunched and tied is a delight 'au naturel '

Indulge yourself and take a peek through the window

The family gardens

An opportunity to share Captain Smith's enchanting English garden. The year is around 1904. It's a lovely warm hazy sunny day. Not a sound except nature's own: the rustling of the leaves in the light summer breeze the seagulls squawking above and the sweet music of the birdsong.

A pony and trap plods by; children play in the street, running to catch it up.

Mel, just 6 years old, is playing, running and chasing Papa's favourite pets, the Borzoi dogs, round and round the garden.

The garden table is laid with a fine lace table cloth, embroidered serviettes and a tiered cake-stand. Mama sits at the table under the veranda with a glass of homemade lemonade, taking shade from the golden sunshine, she watches over Mel playing and laughing in the garden. Grandmama Sarah joins her daughter at the table for afternon tea, she is never too far away from her two girls.

Borzoi dogs Captains favourite

Papa loved the dogs – Borzoi breeds (Russian Hounds) were his favourite, though Mama would complain when she was left to look after them, saying they were a handful and a nuisance while he was away at sea.

When Ted was home, he walked with Mel and his dogs for hours on end. The seashore being just a few yards away from the house, the two of them could run without a care on the golden sand, while the dogs ran into the sea to cool down. What lovely memories for father and daughter.

If you look closely you can just about see the houses on Marine Crescent behind the children in this 1900s photograph.

These gardens are still here today, even more magnificent than before, with matured fruit trees and shrubs. It's a privilege to be able to see these archive pictures.

Golden sands Waterloo

The house immediately left as you walk up the steps here is the Smith family home.

Gardens fronting Marine Crescent

1906 Loving Husband and Father – a family man

The year is 1906 and the family are together at last. Ted has some precious family time in between sailing the Baltic and waiting to sail the Adriatic: what better way to spend time with the family than to enjoy a lovely picnic.

Earlier in the day, Seth, the stable boy prepared the horse and trap, tethering the horse to the railings on Marine Crescent in readiness.

Picnics were very popular with the Victorians, perhaps because it allowed them to escape from the formal dinner rituals.

Ted, Eleanor and Mel were no exception: they enjoyed fine family outings on those rare occasions that Papa Ted was home from sea. Taking the horse and trap to the countryside for a picnic prepared by Kath, the cook, was a delightful afternoon outing. Picnics became treasured memories for mother and daughter, memories to last a lifetime!

Even though he was frequently away for long periods at sea, the relationship between husband and wife remained strong and stable. Eleanor (her preferred name) referred to her husband as 'Ted or Teddy' while Ted spoke of his wife as 'my only dear one'

Papa bestowed great love and fondness on his only daughter. He doted on her; his affectionate names for her were 'gillie' (girly) and 'babs' (baby)

He sent many messages while away to keep his family close in his thoughts, buying gifts from all the many ports, and spending his personal time and space organising parties for his family when he returned home.

Precious brief periods ashore as a family at home

A rare insight into the family man

Walk with me now through to the 'Best Parlour' reserved for special guests – another room that seemed so familiar to me when I first saw it.

Sit yourself down by the fireplace. The room is warm and welcoming as the fire burns fiercely in the hearth.

Imagine if you will, Ted sitting in the large leather chair with exotic cushions

The Smoking Parlour

plumped up for comfort, relaxing smoking his favourite Havana cigars.

Teddy always preferred to smoke his cigar through a cigar holder for effect.

When Ted wanted his peace and quiet he would retire to the study and the rest of the family would not be allowed to enter without his special permission.

*Be **very, very** still as you watch him because in the words of Mel she fondly recalled that after dinner papa would always settle down for a smoke.*

"Cigars" said his daughter, "were his pleasure and one was only allowed to be in the room if one was really really good and absolutely still, so that the blue plume of smoke over his head was not disturbed."

Semi Retirement

Returning home from New York on the Adriatic in 1907, Seth the stable boy would make his way to Lime Street Station to pick up his master to bring him home to his family.

Ted was a popular man, with his grey beard and piercing eyes. He was pleasant, softly spoken, gentle, kind hearted and good humoured; though a stickler for discipline, he earned respect as a leader of men and as master of the house.

Captain Smith had many influential friends whom he met on his travels, not least of whom was American writer, Kate Douglas-Wiggin, authoress of Rebecca of Sunnybrook Farm. She wrote in her autobiography how she had enjoyed visiting his house in England, and loved seeing him in his delightfully happy family life.

A happy life indeed: at the age of 58, Ted was considering retirement. However, it would not be long before he was enticed away from the idea by the Ismay family, his employers, friends and neighbours.

A telephone call to Waterloo 271 would result in a meeting between Captain Smith and the Ismays (owners of the White Star Line): a meeting that changed the course of history. Waterloo is steeped in history. It was once an area for the very rich of Liverpool. Living close to the docks would be beneficial to anyone with merchant or maritime links.

Brokers, Merchants, Mariners and Ship Owners lived in and around Marine Crescent, Beach Lawn, Adelaide Terrace and Marine Terrace. The Ismays lived just 5 minutes walk away in Beach Lawn.

Edward Smith was honoured to be asked to take command of the prestigious Titanic: how could he refuse?

In 1907 the White Star Line headquarters moved to Southampton. Edward took the decision to uproot his family and move from 17 Marine Crescent Liverpool, to be closer to his employers in Southampton.

Many Liverpool men followed him to Southampton, as it was considered an honour to sail with the "Millionaire's Captain", as he became known.

How ironic he wanted to retire after the maiden voyage of Titanic to New York. He wanted to spend more time with his family. This quiet spoken, gentle nobleman who radiated confidence and humour died on 15th April 1912 when the Titanic sank. His body was never recovered. "His last known rallying cry through the megaphone from the bridge was "Be British, my men"

Mother and child 1898/1899

The only known picture of Sarah Eleanor Smith with daughter Mel on her knee while living here. This picture was used on the front cover of The Daily Mirror April 22nd just 7 days after her husband's death. Putting her own personal grief to one side, she wrote:

"To my poor fellow-sufferers: My heart overflows with grief for you all and is laden with sorrow that you are weighed down with this terrible burden that has been thrust upon us. May God be with us and comfort us all"

Background to family life
Domestic staff and their legacy today

In Victorian times, large houses such as these had domestic staff. As we have seen, two servants lived in the main house and a stable boy lived in the stables in the grounds behind the house.

Parlour Maid: Annie Brett, 17, from Cheshire
Domestic Cook: Kate Chambers, 32, from Ireland
Stable Boy: Seth Coxon, 24, from Ireland

Kate's domain was the kitchen, with its oven and baking area perfect for family catering. Here she cooked for the family and, baked food for the day, anything from Victorian sandwich cakes to homemade bread and scones (this fireplace was a hidden gem, just waiting to be discovered)

For many years this was a plastered wall, with no indication of what lay behind it. The room has a solid floor,

Kitchen fireplace / cooking area

an indication that it was once the kitchen. There had to be a fireplace behind the wall: I was compelled to open it up to find out.

I ran a metal detector across the wall until I heard the familiar beep, indicating that there was indeed metal behind the wall. I traced the outline onto the wallpaper.

It was so exciting I was convinced there had to be a cooking range behind the wall. What if there were still kettles and pans or cutlery? How great a discovery for me! I set about breaking through the plaster and uncovered the burnt soldier bricks held up by a metal arch. I had found the fireplace, but disappointingly the range had already been removed.

Stables and coachhouse 1912

There was however, an old brass kettle and trivet: this would have been used by the family all those years ago. It was a fantastic discovery, it made clearing up the mess of the broken plaster, so much easier to bear.

The stables at the rear of the property had their own address, though they are still within the grounds of the main house. The stable boy Seth Coxon resided in Mason Street, Waterloo.

Coachhouse conversion 2012

The building originally had two huge doors: the ponies were kept in the left side, with the trap on the right.

The deeds to the property show a speed limit, *yes, a speed limit* -you can trot your pony no faster than 5 miles per hour on Marine Crescent

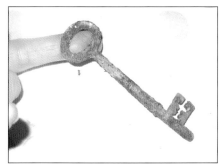

Original key to coachhouse 1819

The well worn steps on the inside wall were used to clamber to the hayloft above. Evidence of hay could still be found when I bought the property. The stable boy Seth lived in the other half of the first floor.

All services to the house, the coal and food deliveries would all be taken in from here, the tradesmen's entrance.

This 180-year-old key, locked the door between the hayloft and the living area of the stables, thankfully I still have the old key.

The floor of the stable was covered in cobble stones, with a trough running down the centre of the floor. There were round holes in the sandstone floor where a wooden post would have been, a place for Seth to tether the ponies.

On the gable end of the stable, there was evidence of a large coal storage, underneath the sandstone steps that led up to Seth's room.

The large oak roof purlins providing support for the main roof of the cottage, have some fascinating markings carved into the wood. These markings remained a mystery and many a person has tried to decipher them.

In 2005 we discovered why the markings were there and what they meant, would you believe that these beams were taken from ships from the Napoleonic War and re-used in the buildings almost 200 years earlier.

The strange markings were actually letters and numbers that had been carved onto the beams. These huge beams were then split into two in order to make transporting them easier. Later they would be used as purlins to hold up the roof of the stables that were being built at the same time as the house.

Opposite the stables were fishermen's cottages: you can still see the wear on the cills, over time they became concave were the fishermen knives would cut into the fish to gut and clean them to sell to markets in East Street Waterloo.

Local dairy cows would graze on the land in front of the stables. Kath the cook would know to fetch the fresh milk, butter and cheese for the day and fresh fish was always a great choice for the Smith family.

As you can see, this is now a lovely residential coach house, a Grade II listed building and a family home converted sympathetically to reflect the period.

Revealed for the first time in 2012 the 100th Anniversary

My life was mapped out ~ It was simply meant to be, the story needed to be told

MY AMAZING STORY – why am I connected? In my life, I've had a handful of significant dreams. Each one has held a deep personal meaning to me.

House 2012

House 1898

As a teenager, I dreamt that I was hurting my father: I actually dreamt my behaviour was killing him. It sounds dramatic, I know, but as much as I loved my father, I was headstrong and stupid. The dream stayed with me the whole of the day, I concluded that my behaviour was affecting him he loved me so much and I was being so hurtful. This typical hormonal teenager changed her ways, became a kinder person and started to treat him with respect. And all because of a dream.

Was someone trying to reach me? I believe so.

Another of my dreams was of my friend Jackie, who died aged 17 from Leukaemia. She was on a bus reaching out to me, I was running after the bus trying to reach out to touch her hand, to pull her off the bus, yet it drove faster: no matter how hard I tried, I couldn't touch her outstretched hand and the bus moved further and further away.

Was someone reaching out to me? Was someone trying to get through to me? I have always believed so. I wrote these dreams in a diary, along with the one I am going to share with you today.

Over thirty years ago, in 1980, while I was still living at home with my parents, I had a dream…

My new home

In February 1988 a friend told of a property for rent. I was 30 years old: you could be forgiven for thinking, it's about time she flew the nest!

I remember the day as if it were yesterday! I absolutely fell in love with the place.

You know when you look to buy a house and you get that warm feeling as you walk in? Well that was me: I really had to have this place. Nothing else would do. With its huge windows, it was so bright and sunny, perfect, I felt I could be happy here. I rang and pestered the agent who showed me the flat, until he was tired of hearing my voice. My persistence paid off: I was given the keys in March 1988.

Oh, but I really did fall in love with the place: friends remarked on the difference in me, I put that down to having my independence at last… The property was quite a strange configuration though. It was very long, each room was behind the other, no rooms left to right, just straight back in a line.

I soon discovered that the blue threadbare carpet in the living room was actually cut into bits like a jigsaw: it tried its best to stay in place on the floor, but I guess the 'bits' had a mind of their own.

The kitchen: what kitchen? Two corner shelves and a Belfast sink. The sink had a cold tap that would stick, and the pressure from the tap would have the water jumping over the sink onto the floor. I remember crying uncontrollably that first night because, try as I might, I simply didn't have the strength to turn it off. I thought there would be a flood!

Dad came to my rescue, taking the bus: one hour later my knight in shining armour turned up with the wrench, fixed the tap and then dried my tears. Fancy a cuppa, dad…?

Still, I didn't mind these little quirks: it was just lovely and had a great homely feel about it. With just an uncomfortable settee filled with horsehair and the proverbial spring cutting through the material, a small black and white TV sitting on the mantelpiece because I didn't have a table, craning my neck to watch it – oh yes, I did also have a bed, but that was about all.

Diane and her young daughter, Vicky, who lived in the upstairs of the house, became my very close friends and companions: we shared many good times here. What more could I ask for, I really couldn't have been happier.

1989: The bubble is about to burst.

I was at work, when Diane rang to tell me an estate agent had been sent to value the whole property by the owner, Mrs Ewart. The owner lived in the south of England and rarely ventured up north. If she sold the house, I was going to lose my home. My world was caving in: I was about to lose everything. I rang the estate agents, saying that as a tenant of the property could they tell me what it had been valued at? As I was merely a tenant, the estate agent refused to reveal the value to me. I was desperate and clutching at straws. I said, "OK, if I ring you today and ask you to value my property, would you ask me to prove I owned it". "No," was the reply. "Either tell me the value or I will request that you come back to value it", I said. A short while later, I had the information I required, there were two figures. Two valuations: one with the tenants in, one with the tenants out.

The house was to be sold from underneath our feet for £80k* providing the tenants moved out and the place was empty.

However there was a 2nd valuation of £40k* if a new buyer was prepared to buy with the tenants remaining in the house.

We decided to try our luck and go in with the lowest valuation of £40k

After all we had lived here for a while and had never seen the owner Mrs Ewart. She was unlikely to take too much interest, this was just one of many properties on her huge portfolio.

We instructed our solicitor to go in with the low valuation of £40k*, she wrote that her 'client' was interested in the property.

Unknown to Mrs Ewart, we the tenants, were infact the 'client' we held our breath... To our amazement, the gamble paid off, the offer was accepted and we got our wish at a fraction of the price. Oh boy, did we party that day…

*The figures shown are for illustration purposes only and don't reflect the actual price paid, what they DO reflect is that one valuation was half of the other. There were three flats, two on the ground floor and one on the first. Diane and I agreed to buy the house between us, each owning our own section. Diane owned the whole top of the house while I owned the ground floor.

How I learned this was the Captain's family home
From Titanic Film Researchers

In the early 1990s, researchers for the epic film Titanic arrived at the house. They revealed that Captain Smith had lived here and were exploring the possibility of filming the opening scenes of the film in the house. "Would you be interested in allowing this to happen?" they asked. "Of course!" was our response..

1997 epic film Titanic

WOW... WHAT A DISCOVERY

Surprised, excited, bewildered and intrigued, with my new found knowledge, I read up at the library, everything I could find out about the local history and in particular about this house and who lived here.

• Census records
• Birth dates
• Gores Street Directory
• Kelly's Directory
• Pictures and maps
• New paper articles and much more

Gores street directory

Sure enough, he lived here from 1898 – 1907, telephone number Waterloo 271.

It was a talking point for many years to come, Captain Smith and his family truly did live in this house. Diane and I felt quite honoured to be living here.

After 15 years living and owning the house between us, my friend Diane decided it was time to move on to a new home. In 2004 she sold her half of the house to me. At last I owned the complete house. I was now able to invest some serious time and money into the property.

The newly acquired part of the house needed a little TLC, I started the work. The master bedroom had no fire surround, just the opening were a fire had been. I was intrigued. Every room had a marble fire surround so what happened to this one?

Had Diane had it removed? No she said, she hadn't removed anything.

Convinced I had seen a fire surround there, I said, "*but there was a surround there remember, it was small and had a white marble surround*" I was able to describe it in detail: moreover, I was describing a marble fireplace that was smaller than the others in the house.

She insisted there had never been a marble fire surround since she had lived in the flat: there was a fireplace fire but no surround. I was shown photographs with just a gas fire against the chimney breast, so why is it that I can describe the missing marble fireplace with such detail?

Restoration

Restoring the house to its former glory was a challenge, a huge responsibility, and a privilege. It took many years of love and hard work, the results of which are there for all to see. Once it had been restored, I wanted to share the news that Captain Smith had lived here with his family: but how to go about it? I tried on many occasions to apply for a Blue Plaque from English Heritage, only to find they no longer work outside of the London area.

Not one to be beaten

In 2005 the city of Liverpool was gearing up to celebrate its rich maritime legacy. The 'Year of the Sea' was a full year-long celebration, which included the Clipper round the world yacht race and the bicentennial celebration of the Battle of Trafalgar. The maritime themed year was part of celebrating Britain as a seafaring nation, highlighting its enviable maritime heritage.

What better time to highlight my plight? It was important to let the public know: it was vital for Liverpool heritage. I wrote a heartfelt plea, to all the dignitaries: everyone received an email, with the headline: **Year of the Sea – Maritime History Lost**

The response was immediate, it should be recognised as part of our local heritage. The plaque was finally erected some two months later. A long journey for me…

Coincidence – or just lucky?

Over 8 years ago on holiday in the Isle of Wight, I was rummaging around an antique shop, when my friend spotted a newspaper from 1912. The front page had Eleanor Smith with daughter Mel. It was a copy of an original I had no real interest in it.

The true significance of this didn't hit me at the time until I returned home. That photograph would have been taken while she lived in the house. I regretted not buying the newspaper, but too late to look back.

I never forgot that picture and when I began to write this story, my interest in finding the photograph grew in strength.

Last year in September 2011, while browsing around a market stall in Liverpool, I got chatting to the stall holder 'Barbara', we talked about a painting I had at home that was painted by a famous artist from the 1800's. I wanted to know more about it. Did it have a value other than my love for it?

She suggested I took it to a city auctioneer, we agreed to meet the following Monday at Cato Crane auction house, were you can view items prior to the sale which takes place the following day. I took a look around it was a fantastic place filled with memorabilia a really fascinating place to root for antiques.

Amongst the wonderful array of cigarette cases, ancient books, furniture, pictures and mirrors, an old A4 tatty blue folder caught my attention, it was just about noticeable from behind a large set of encyclopaedias.

Why I was drawn to this folder is just another amazing feature of my story. The contents had been hidden away from the world for 100 years, just waiting to be discovered.

Inside that plain tattered folder numbered 'item 184', was the very newspaper I had seen all those years ago in the Isle of Wight. The Daily Mirror dated April 22nd 1912 with Eleanor Smith and her daughter Mel on her knee on the front page. In fact there were 6 ORIGINAL newspapers in all dating from April 17th to April 22nd. Eleanor and Mel were beckoning me to them, waiting to be taken home.

Returning to the auction house the following day, my heart was in my mouth. (What if someone else wanted them)

During the auction I watched in horror as a man opened the folder and handled my precious newspapers, inside me I was screaming PUT THEM DOWN their mine, Item number 182... 183... then item 184, with a deep breath I placed my bid and to my amazement I wasn't challenged. I can't express how I felt when I won the bid.

They were going back to where they belonged. 17 Marine Crescent.

The Author

Before you go on to learn about my dream, ask yourself this, was it another coincidence or was I drawn to this place by spirit.

The dream revealed

I mentioned earlier that my connection to this house was made in 1970 - 18 years before I had ever set eyes on it.

In 1970 whilst living at home with my parents, I had an amazing dream, one that would stay with me for the rest of the day. I felt so strongly about it, I was compelled to put pen to paper. These are the very words I wrote in my diary:

Went to see a flat today, I just fell in love with it, I just had to have it

It had a weird layout though, the rooms went one behind the other, straight in a line.

A living room with a bedroom immediately behind, a kitchen behind the bedroom and a bathroom behind the kitchen, each room behind the other in a straight line.

As I left the flat, I walked down the path and turned to take another look. I noted how the large open windows reminded very much of a 'shop front' I want this so badly, I love this place, make them an offer

OFFER THEM £20,000*

My entry complete, the diary was then filed away and forgotten about.

I really never gave this a second thought until the day the penny dropped.

This house WAS familiar to me, the flat I loved and lived in DID go back and back in a straight line, the large window is similar to a SHOP FRONT window.

I took out my diary and I was amazed at what I had written all those years earlier.

Diane and I paid £40,000* to purchase the house from Mrs Ewart, so you see, my actual offer was £20,000* just as my dream had predicted 18 years earlier!

* The figures shown are for illustration purposes only and do not represent the actual price paid.

I will save the last word for my beautiful mother Ivy, who one day made this wise observation:

'This house was just waiting for someone to love it'

She was so right, It was simply meant to be.

Oh yes: by the way ~ my name?

Its 'Rose'

I hope you enjoyed sharing my experience and my home as much as my friends and family do when the garden is shared with the people I love, Just as it has been from 1898 to 2012.

2012 LIVERPOOL The Costa Concordia ran aground off the island of Giglio on Jan. 13 2012. My thoughts are with those people affected by this tragedy.